THE COMPLETE DETOX GUIDE

DETOX
YOURSELF

kol tov

Introduction

KOL TOV Author

We live in a very chaotic world. We also live in a very polluted world. You probably don't need me to remind you of this fact. There are all sorts of pollution available and, thankfully, the United States is one of the world's leaders in cutting down on physical pollution.

I am, of course, talking about pollutants that make their way into our air, water, and food. The Environmental Protection Agency, despite whatever issues it have, has done a generally good job of protecting citizens from physical and chemical pollutants.

The same can be said of the US Food and Drug Administration. Thanks to their vigilance, they have done an outstanding job making sure that most of the food items that make their way to our table are generally safe. Of course, there are certain issues that we can nitpick over like GMO and certain types of chemical residues. Still, it can't be denied that, by and large, the US and other developed countries are fairly well-protected against standard the sources of pollution.

If you don't believe me, just hop on a plane and go to Beijing, China. The difference in air quality, water quality, and food safety is like day and night. This is not a slam on China because they are making great progress in tightening regulations but it has to be said that when it comes to protecting its citizens, the developed world has done a fairly good job.

This is why a lot of people are kind of confused as to with the whole idea of detoxification has gained a lot of traction lately. After all, federal, local, and state regulatory bodies have done a fairly good job of projecting people from chemical toxins and physical threats to their safety.

If only things were that simple. You have to understand that the toxins that afflict modern people aren't just restricted to chemical forms. Chemical toxins and pollutants are very easy to screen. They're very easy to detect. And, yes, they are very easy to prevent and treat. The same goes with diseases.

Forget what you've heard before. Detoixfication is not just a simple matter of going on a juice diet or going without food for an extended period of time. It goes beyond that.

If anything else, it means that you're going to have to re-examine the kind of life you are living and the kind of life you have built for yourself. You can quickly discover that a lot of the things that you choose to believe to be true are actually making you sick. At the very least, they're not helping you perform at peak levels.

This book teaches people from all walks of life to conduct a complete detox of their life. This detox regimen applies across the board. Whether you are suffering from mental toxins or you're struggling with spiritual pollutants or you are faced with the standard physical adulterants that weigh you down and drag you back, this book has something for you.

By using a holistic method to detox, you will be able to live life to the fullest. If you are in any way, shape, or form unhappy, frustrated, or feeling stuck in your life, it is because you have allowed certain things to weigh you down. This is just as bad as being addicted to drugs. This is just problematic as struggling with chemical pollution. Just because you can see it, smell it, taste it or hear it, it doesn't mean it doesn't exist.

You know full well the effects of mental pollution. This book enables you to break free from all of that so you can live up to your fullest potential. All of us are on this planet for a purpose. The sad truth is that we have allowed certain mindsets to get the better of us and this has clouded our view of what our purpose should be.

It is no surprise that the vast majority of us are simply going through the motions. You go from hour to hour, day to day, and moment to moment with really no clear direction as to why we're here. This book cuts through all that fog and enables you to bask in the sunlight of purpose, clarity, and meaning.

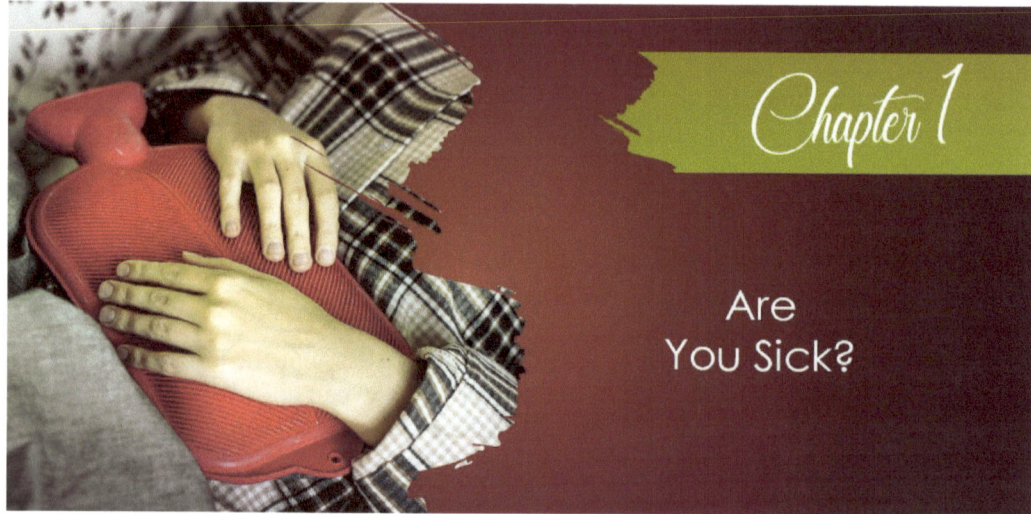

In western cultures, sickness has traditionally been defined as physical, medical or mental. While western psychology and psychiatry have progressed quite a bit over the years, there's still a long held impression in the medical community regarding the mind-body connection.

Unfortunately, given what's going on and the trends in general society both in the developed and developing world, traditional definitions of sickness are short sided and all too limited. It doesn't do any good to define sickness in very narrow biochemical terms.

As western medicine dug deeper and deeper into a biochemical germ based or pathogen-centric definition of medicine, a lot is lost in translation. While it has made big strides in bridging the effect of psychology and overall stress on physical health, there's still a lot to be desired.

The bottom line is that we can learn quite a bit from Hindu traditions or eastern traditions that deal with the concept of sickness. In those traditions, sickness is defined holistically. They're more likely to put a lot of stock on the concept of spiritual pollution, emotional stress, interpersonal sickness and other factors that have a strong impact on the human psyche and overall sense of well being.

These factors then manifest themselves in actual physical illness or substandard physical performance. You may be perfectly "healthy" in biochemical terms. All your tests may come out clean. But your doctor will still be stumped as to why you feel lousy all the time.

There are a lot of people who have all sorts of symptoms similar to lupus or auto immune diseases. But when the blood chemistry tests come in, they should be getting a clean health. Physically speaking, there's nothing wrong with them. But there they are, suffering. Feeling like they are at their ropes end.

Ask yourself, "Am I sick?" There's nothing wrong with asking this question. There's no shame involving this. Remember, the worst thing that you can do is to pretend that you don't have a problem. How can you find the answer when you're fooling yourself into thinking that there's no problem?

Chapter 2

Rediscovering The "Wholistic" Person

Since traditional definitions of sickness are too restricted to the physical and biochemical realms, it is not a surprise that a lot of modern people can't get the relief that they desire from psychopharmaceutical drugs and chemical based medicine in general.

In fact when you look at the top 10 medications prescribed in the United States and Western Europe, anti-anxiety, anti-depressant and anti-hypertensive medications are almost always in the top 5 or top 10. You can bank on them being present year after year.

There's something wrong here. Even though we have been bombarding these illnesses with a wide range of chemical cocktails over the years, we're still sicker and sicker and we pay more and more money and there seems to be no solution in sight.

You are more than your physical parts

A lot of this existential angst and its matching physical symptoms is due to the fact that people are more than their physical parts. They're not just a collection of blood pressure readings, blood sugar levels, uric acid tests scores and a wide range of biochemical indicators.

All of these may come out clean and fall well within "normal range". But that doesn't mean that people will stop feeling lousy, stressed and suffering from "brain fog". This is due to the fact that if people want to get well and step away from just choosing to survive, but to actually live fully, they have to look at their complete being in "wholistic" terms.

What does "wholistic" mean? Just as your mind is composed of more than your brain, your life and overall health is composed of more than just your body. We're not even talking about the additional dimensions of psychological and emotional health.

We're also talking about how you get along with other people, how you look at yourself in the grand scheme of things, what your sense of personal meaning and purpose are, what you choose to eat, how you construct your day, what kind of environments you find yourself in.

In other words, we go beyond the physical. We escape the narrow confines of the biochemical foundation of your life. While biochemistry and your physical body are absolutely important, they are not the complete picture. Far from it.

Rediscovering the power of the whole person

When we start looking at people as more that just what we can see, we will start making progress as to actual effective treatment. Whatever it is you are suffering from, whatever physical manifestations of stress or a lack of purpose may be hounding you, whatever aches and pains you may experience, all of these can be addressed with a wholistic approach.

Chapter 3

Reclaim Parts Of Yourself That You Have Overlooked Or Forgotten About

There are many different parts of the human psyche. There are many different faces that make up who we are. When you leave your home, you are different people to the different individuals you meet. You're somebody's brother or sister, then you are somebody's boss or somebody's employee or somebody's contractor. On and on it goes.

We're different people to the people we find ourselves in different situations. We may be in the same place, but at different times, we're different people or we are different people at the same time, but at different places.

In other words, we're different people in terms of times and space. What happens to these identities? It's as if you're wearing all these different masks with different angles on them. How do you reconcile all of this?

Unfortunately, as I've mentioned, we live in a world of specialization. So we're forced to slice and dice and pick and choose. This does a big disservice to just the rich tapestry of all identities and capabilities.

There is power in wholeness

When you choose to live with full integrity, this means you reconnect with everything that defines you. In other words, integrity means you connect the potential with what is manifesting, you reconcile what you desire with what you are producing.

This requires introspection and a whole lot of honesty. This means you reconnect with everything that defines you. There's the physical you, the biochemical you, the emotional you, the spiritual you, the psychological you, the cultural you, the relational you. I can go on and on.

Unfortunately, a lot of us just focus on one thing and one thing alone. In fact, there's a lot of us who define ourselves as one dimensional human beings. If you need proof of this, go to a party and talk to people and the first thing out of most people's mouths is what they do for a living.

They would say, "Hi! My name is Jerry. I'm an attorney." or "Hello! My name is Mindy. I'm a doctor at the nearby hospital." or "My name is Albert and I work for Microsoft." People tend to define themselves in a one dimensional way. We always try to connect with some larger phenomena that somehow casts a shadow on our own identity.

For example, when somebody introduces himself or herself as working for Facebook, what's the first thing that comes to your mind? Facebook has a brand and there's a value judgment there that's very different from somebody stepping up to you and saying, "Hey! My name is Joe. I'm an executive at Starbucks."

In the case of Joe, there are 2 things going on. When he says hes an executive, that brings to mind certain ideas. And when they say "Starbucks", that also brings a whole other set of issues.

Unfortunately, a lot of us are just focused on one thing. We become one dimensional. It's as if we're walking cartoons. And the worst part to all of this is we don't even realize it. If we're lucky we get up to 2 or even 3 of these factors in terms of us defining ourselves. That doesn't even come close.

By restricting ourselves to the kind of identity we have, we let go of a lot of our connections to the rest of the natural world. This is why we suffer. This is why we feel incomplete. This is why we feel so susceptible to stress, to changing to situations and to the vagaries of life.

This is why we struggle.

The first step you could take to fully detoxify yourself is to step out of the binary divisions that you have used to define reality prior to this point. This is a mouthful. I admit this is pretty heavy duty stuff. It definitely requires a commitment. It is not something that you can take lightly. This is not something that you can casually screw around with.

It's not like you can adopt all of this instantly with a full assurance that things will be okay. It takes a lot of work. Just as you have been programmed throughout the years to think of yourself within the universe in a certain way, it takes some time and consistent focus to unwind all of that programming.

Here are just some basic ideas to think about as you seek to detoxify yourself on more than just a physical or biochemical level.

Overcome the "either or" mindset

Our modern mindset is all about division, as I've mentioned in the previous chapter. This mindset is all about finding some sort of primacy over one aspect at the expense of others. It's the whole idea of the male over the female, the rational over the intuitive, black over white, science over faith.

The problem with this is that it's all about one thing over another. There's little space for a gray area. There's little space for intuition, hunches, nuance. While there's a lot to be said for the focus division and separation brings, a lot is also lost especially when a lot of our basic needs have already been taken care of.

A sense of lack in a time of plenty

One thing that always blows my mind is the prevalence of loneliness, isolation and desperation in parts of the world that can be truly called lands of plenty.

Whether we're talking about Australian, New Zealand, Canada, western Europe, United States or all points in between, there are many areas in this world where physical needs I'm talking about having enough calories to make it from day to day have been more than taken care of.

It won't be an exaggeration to say that many people in these places live on the lap of luxury. They have access to many things that even their ancestors would find truly amazing and stupendous. But here we are, with massive rates of disconnection, divorce, addiction, perhaps even crime or self harm.

This is one of life's riches ironies. We live in a modern world where a lot of people feel that they have so little of what truly matters. Yet if they choose to look around them, they are surrounded by abundance.

Diagnosing REAL poverty

Did you know that millionaires kill themselves all the time? I'm not just talking about Kate Spade, Anthony Bourdain, Robin Williams or any other fairly well off celebrity that we've all heard of. I'm talking about relatively faceless, high net worth individuals who choose to pull the plug on their lives.

They have everything to live for. But unfortunately, they have nothing to live from. There is no shortage of people who have 7 or even 8 figures in the bank killing themselves in many ways. I'm not just talking about suicide. I'm also talking about drug addiction. That's a form of suicide.

There's a sickness going on. We're living in polluted times. A lot of this has to do with the mindset that we have. And unless you are going to see this for what it is, which is pollution, we will continue to be blind to it. unfortunately we'll continue to live with its effects.

It doesn't feel good to think that you're just going around in circles that you put in all this time, effort and energy only to end up in the same place. It would be great to feel that there is a purpose for your life and that you are actually going somewhere.

Unfortunately, as the years go by and as technology evolves, the more connected we become and the faster data processes our lives and our impulse, the more disconnected we feel. Back in the day, it was weird to feel lonely in a crowd. Now, you can see street scenes all over the place of people looking at their mobile devices all at once. They're all connected and disconnected at the same time.

We're all living in our own little world. But that world is disjointed, private. We're, at the same time, collaborating through all this technology while at the same time stewing in our own personal mental prisons.

A lot of this can be traced to the fact that we have let certain pollutants get the better of us.

Chapter 5

Be Aware Of Your Pollutants

What pollutants hold you back and drag you down? What pollutants do you need to detoxify yourself of. This is where things get a little tricky because it's very easy to define "pollutant" in terms of biochemistry.

Heavy metals are pollutants. Mercury is a nasty pollutant. Excess carbon dioxide in the air as well as methane are well known pollutants. It's very easy to think of pollutants in strictly physical or biochemical terms.

Either we insist that we see it like in the form of sludge, oil spills or chemical contamination, or detect it in some way or other like in the form of escaping gas. But even if we were to define pollutants in these rather broad terms, they don't go far enough.

You see, pollutants take many forms. And until and unless we can open our minds to the definition of these pollutants in terms of a wholistic perspective, we sell our self short. We unnecessarily restrict the problem and it should come as no surprise that our solutions also come up short.

What follows is a wholistic definition of pollutants. Until and unless you can wrap your mind around these, the real solution won't come. You'll still feel stuck. You'll still feel that somethings missing in your life. You'll still have a tough time making sense of things because you constantly find yourself comparing yourself to others.

You have to have a more expansive view of pollutants so you can go through a truly effective detox program.

Limiting beliefs

Limiting beliefs have done more harm for people than any kind of chemical or physical substance. Think about it. If you can see a sign that says "Biohazard" or you see a radiation warning sign or some sort of chemical spill danger sign, you'd back off. It's pretty straight forward. After all, these are physical pollutants.

Not so with limiting beliefs. In fact, a lot of people think that their limiting beliefs are part of who they are. I can't even begin to tell you how many people I've come across who are extremely negative, caustic and toxic.

When I talk to these individuals, they basically tell me, "This is who I am. This is all I could be. I was born this way." This is a problem. Unlike physical pollutants, which you can easily see or physically detect through your 5 senses, mental and spiritual pollutants are more pernicious. They cling to you. Kind of like a bad case of BO.

And just like BO, the longer you have it, the less you smell it. Your limiting beliefs, sooner or later, define you. Remember, your limiting beliefs is your personal filter for reality. It's like a pair of glasses you put on when you look at everything around you.

Of course, depending on the color of your lenses, the appearance of your world can dramatically change. Before you know it, you assume that the world really looks like this. But it turns out that you can change those lenses.

What makes limiting belief so dangerous?

So what? We all have these "attitude sunglasses". Isn't one just as valid as another? Isn't that part of the diversity of life? What's the big deal about limiting beliefs?

Well, limiting beliefs are dangerous precisely because they trick you into thinking that they come from you. You are under the impression that your limiting belief is just restricted to you, that it's part of who you are, that it's the product of you living your life.

We make all sorts of grand justifications and explanations about our limiting beliefs. It's kind of like being bound in handcuffs and you spend a lot of time decorating your handcuffs. Maybe you'd be better off realizing that you're wearing handcuffs no matter how beautiful those handcuffs are. Maybe the better approach would be to think about how to take off those handcuffs.

But unfortunately, we reach our point with our limiting beliefs that we believe they're part of our identity and we simply can not let go of them. In fact, some people take this to the next level and say they will die without these beliefs.

They draw neat, tidy lines of limitation around their complete life. Who they can be, the things they can do, the people they can hang out with and what their future could look like.

The reality behind limiting beliefs

What if I told you that your limiting beliefs are chosen. You don't have to keep saying to yourself that you are dumb or you don't have what it takes or that you have no money. You don't have to keep saying to yourself that you're unlucky or that you're ugly or too old to get married.

Just as you are able to choose them in the first place, you can choose to let them go. At first, you took on a limiting belief casually. You kind of picked it up as you were moving along. But the more you lived your life and the more you believed in that belief and the more you chose it to filter your reality of the outside world, the stronger it became. It became harder and harder to let go.

Celebrate your power of choice

The key to detoxifying yourself from limiting beliefs and other forms of spiritual pollution is to rediscover your power of choice. I know you're going to have a tough time taking this in. But you have a choice.

You may think that you're a victim. You may think that your life is already set. You may think that there's really not much you can do about your life. You're definitely welcome to think these things. But they are not reality.

You have to understand that victims cannot choose. Life simply inflicts oppression on them. They have no choice in the matter. I'm happy to report that you are never a victim. You can always choose. Even if somebody's inflicting harm on you, you can choose how to respond.

If and only if you accept this fact, then you will be on your way to becoming a victor. You know what a victor is? It is somebody who makes things happen instead of somebody who constantly asks in desperation and helplessness "What happened?"

The good news is you can detoxify yourself from limiting beliefs and other spiritual pollutants. But you must take the first necessary step.

You must first realize that you chose your life and you can choose another kind of life.

Chapter 6

From Victim To Victor:
The Detox Path

Are you a victim? You can be completely honest. I know that in our society, it's not exactly a good thing when people come out and say that they feel like they're victims. But if you want to fully detoxify from all the pollutants in your life, you have to come clean. You have to be authentic and true to yourself.

If none of this makes sense, ask yourself the following questions. If you answer yes to at least 2 of these, then chances are high that you are a victim or, at least, you consider yourself one.

Do you think you're entitled to life being fair?
Does it seem like everybody misunderstands you?
Does it seem like no matter how hard you try, things just don't work out because you're unlucky?
Does it seem like people are conspiring against you or just don't like you?
Does it appear that you don't have the skills you need to get ahead?
Are other people to blame for your childhood?
Are other people to blame because you're not happy today?
Is your boss holding you down by paying you less than you are worth?
Do people in your relationships have a tough time discovering "the real you"?

If at least 2 of these questions ring true to you or apply to you, chances are you are a victim or you think you are a victim.

Claim your victim status

It's very hard to solve a problem if you believe you don't have one. For example, it's very hard to get an alcoholic to stop drinking if they don't think they're an alcoholic. If they have no problems with how much they drink and what they drink, then they're not going to get any better. There's no problem to solve.

The same analysis applies to your self victimization. If you think you're like a victim, then now is the time to get to that moment of truth. You have to be clear with yourself. This means you have to be completely honest with yourself.

At this point, you may be working with the assumption that you are some sort of victim. Ask yourself, "Am I really a victim or am I just acting like one? Do I think like one? Do I understand the world like a victim?"

Please understand that this is not blame finding. I'm not trying to make you feel bad about yourself or put you on the spot. But until and unless you can accept the fact that you've been playing the victim game or whipping out the victim card at every opportunity, things are not going to change.

Your life is definitely not going to change if you keep this up. Own up to this. Is this what you're doing? Do you see yourself as some sort of victim? Do you always see yourself as the underdog? Do you see yourself as the person that things are happening to instead of the person who is actively making things happen?

You have to be completely clear here because if there's any kind of victimization, you have to look at it straight in the eye and accept that this is happening. If you are in any kind of state of denial, progress is impossible.

How can there be progress when you deny that there's even a problem in the first place? You won't be able to fix what you need to fix.

Detox step #1: Stop blaming other people in situations beyond your control

When you blame other people, you're actually handing power over your life to those people. Think about that. This logically makes sense. Since you say that they caused your problem, then this automatically means they will have the solution.

You've spent all this time blaming other people and unwittingly took all the power to change your circumstances from your hands and placed it in theirs. Obviously, this is not empowering. This is not helping things. This is only going to make your life worse and worse.

Sure, it feels good because you have some sort of emotional release. Who doesn't feel good when the weight of responsibility is lifted off their shoulders? When you feel like you're a victim, you don't have to change. Other people have to change.

Doesn't that feel good? But the problem is you pay a very big price for that sense of emotional release or even your sense of vindication. That sense of vindication you feel when you blame other people, like your father abusing you or your mother making you feel like garbage, comes at a very high price because you rob yourself of the power to make something out of yourself.

Of course, most people don't phrase things this way. But in operational terms, psychologically, this is the effect. Here's the truth. The people you're constantly blaming? They're gone! Seriously! They're living their lives. Maybe they have new families. Perhaps they've moved on, as traumatic as that experience may have been for both of you.

They're not, in any way, shape or form, feeling your anger, hate and resentment. The only person taking the brunt of all that emotional damage is you. Stop beating yourself up. Stop rehearsing that very painful image of a traumatic past. Nobody's being helped by this.

Take ownership today

Take ownership of your life. I know this is easier said than done. But you have to do it. Not your father who was emotionally absents, not your mother who may have been domineered, not your ex boyfriend who may have screwed with your head, not your girlfriend who may have betrayed you, but you.

Say to yourself, "Yes. I've lived my life as a victim. For all this time, I've blamed other people. Now, I'm going to stop blaming others. Instead, I'm going to say it's my fault. It's my responsibility. I own this." You have to make yourself say these and you have to mean it.

Until you are able to say that you totally own your life and you made everything in it happen or you've let it happen, nothings going to change. Please understand that everything that happens to your life was either chosen by you or you let it happen. Why? Because you could always control how you respond.

As you read this book, a bolt of lighting might hit you. Obviously, you didn't cause it. But I can guarantee you that you have total control about how you respond to that unfortunate circumstance. Retake that sense of ownership you have over your life because that power to choose is the only real power you have.

Here's the good news. The power to choose is the fountain head of all possibility in your life. Reclaim that power and you can turn your life around.

Unless it hurts, it's not real

Quick warning: it's very easy to just go through some sort of intellectual laundry list of the things that you should own up to. Everything that I've said prior to this point is very easy to intellectually compartmentalize and treat like some sort of academic information.

Many people do a good job of lying to themselves because they just go down the list of all their screw ups. At the end of the day, it doesn't change them. They intellectually accept these. But they don't develop a sense of emotional urgency.

In other words, it doesn't cut close to home. Deep down inside, on an emotional level, there's still this hermetically sealed compartment in their mind about who truly is at fault. You can say to yourself that you allowed your father to harm you. You could say to yourself that you have allowed your mother run your life and make you feel miserable.

You can repeat that in your head like a mantra. But the problem is until it reaches on a deep and emotional level where you completely own it, nothing will change. There are so many people out there who have gone through psychiatric counseling who know their issues. But they refuse to change because whatever revelations that they have come across remain lists in their head.

These truths must burn. How bad? You have to make a fool out of yourself. You have to feel that you have let yourself down. You have to feel that you've really screwed yourself over. In other words, you have to stop running away from the impact of these emotions.

Put simply, you have to do things that you have been fearing for all this time. The good news is once it hurts, then you know that this laundry list of realizations is true. If it doesn't hurt or it seems so glib or inconvenient, then you're just playing mind games with yourself. You're just wasting your time.

There's absolutely no detoxification happening.

Chapter 7

The Most Important Emotional Detox You Need To Take

Do an audit of all your beliefs and take ownership of them. Human lives are made up of beliefs. Our beliefs are not just these mental clouds that float through our minds with no effect. They're not just conversational notions that we talk about from time to time with absolutely no impact on our daily waking lives. No.

Our beliefs define our lives. They are the cement that holds our lives together. Everything about you, from the way you wear your hair, your choice of clothing, the way you talk, even the condition of your skin are all products of what you choose to believe about yourself deep down inside.

If you believe that you're a certain type of person, then this means that you believe that you are capable of certain things and not others. Don't think that these beliefs just stay in your head. They have an impact on what you choose to think about, how you interpret reality, the things you choose to perceive or even remember and what you feel about your interpretations of reality.

In other words, they have a real impact on how you process reality. This manifests in the things that you say, the things you feel and the things that you do. In other words, they impact your choices. List these beliefs out.

Please understand that it doesn't matter whether they're "good" or "bad". This is no time to be judging them. Just list down all your beliefs. Do a mental purge. Write down the first thing that comes to mind and keep writing until you run out of ideas. Take your time.

Work from where you are

It's very easy to say that you should let go of limiting beliefs. It's very easy to view your life as a simple menu with certain disagreeable items on it. It is tempting to think that to improve your life, you just need to cut out the disagreeable items and you can move on.

It doesn't work that way, sadly enough. Whatever garbage, poison or cancer you think your life may have is simply a matter of interpretation. As the old saying goes, one man's garbage is another man's treasure. It all depends on your point of view.

That traumatic experience that you think robbed you of your childhood might actually be the cathartic experience somebody else needs to become a winner in life. Two completely different people who undergo the same traumatic experience often come out in two totally different ways.

Understand that your interpretation of your reality is encapsulated in your belief. It's only as negative as your willingness to view it that way. You interpret your experiences as negative and guess what happens next. That's right! These experiences have a negative effect on how you feel and think about things.

Ultimately, they have an effect on how you do things. There is a better way. Instead of simply just cutting all these out and letting go, there is a better approach. Let's get real here. It's almost impossible to cut out your past. It's as if you can take some sort of amnesia capsule. It doesn't work that way.

You will always have your past. Those experiences happen. These are facts. They're not going to go away any time soon. The better approach would be to "rearrange your mental furniture".

Step #1: Reinterpret your beliefs

Beliefs don't come out of nowhere. There are certain facts in your background or in your life and certain experiences that support those beliefs. It's as if they give oxygen to those beliefs and these facts maintain your beliefs. Indeed, these facts even make them grow.

What if you can take whatever sustains your beliefs and interpret those facts differently? Instead of your belief grinding you down and making you feel like garbage, reinterpret these facts so they empower you and make you feel that life is possible once again.

Choose to look at these facts from totally different perspectives and choose to believe that you don't have to live your life living in some sort of tightly defined, neat little box.

Step #2: Detoxify your belief interpretation system

Please remember that beliefs don't come out of nowhere. They are being sustained by external experiences. These are called facts. To pretend otherwise is to basically set yourself up for a massive let down.

Whatever progress you achieve would be short lived. Sooner or later, your old habitual patterns will come back and you end up where you started. That's a dead end. Don't even try. For this detox step to work, you have to detoxify the way you interpret your personal reality.

Ask yourself, is this the only way to interpret these facts? Is this the only reading? Or is there something more neutral or, better yet, something more positive?

Follow these steps to detoxify your mindset

Ask yourself the following questions, "What am I really perceiving?" When you ask yourself this question, you force yourself to be more objective. This means that you look at things both at face value and also in terms of alternatives.

Next, ask yourself, "What do I normally assume about the things that I experience?" When you do this, you're basically asking yourself, "Is there any other way to interpret the things that I am perceiving aside from my habitual interpretations or responses?"

You're giving yourself an out. You're giving yourself and alternative. Look for a neutral interpretation or, if you can do it, a positive read on the objective stimuli that you are observing from the real world.

Identify an empowering interpretation and repeat it at every opportunity

Practice makes perfect. It's very hard for many people to adopt a new habit precisely because they feel they don't have time. The way you think about the world and your place in it form a big part of your mental habits.

A key part of mental detox is to let go of this through the repetition of a more empowering interpretation. The moment an image of your abusive father comes to mind, you can always try to override it by saying, "Well, my father was always working. When he came home, he was dead tired. He didn't have time to screw around with kids who did not appreciate him."

Try to put yourself in the shoes of your mother who you felt, throughout all this time, was domineering and controlling. Is there any other possible explanation why she behaved the way she did?

Put yourself in the shoes of your ex girlfriend who stabbed you in the back by sleeping with your best friend. Is there a possible justification for that? I know that none of this is easy because a lot of this involves facts that you may have been trying to run away from for so long.

But until and unless you confront them and, most importantly, look at alternative readings based out of compassion or empathy, nothings going to change. Your old mental interpretation of these triggers will keep feeding into your mental habits.

Repeat it until it sets in

Repeat your new interpretation until it sets in. Keep repeating it until it becomes habitual. How do you know it's habitual? When it becomes your automatic response. That mental image flashes, for example, your father leaving your family, and then the new interpretation comes in.

When you can see daylight between how you reacted in the past, which is anger, resentment and self blame, to something more positive, then you're not trying hard enough. Keep repeating it until you see that distinction.

This kind of thing is not going to happen over night. But the good news is that it does assume some form of momentum. Eventually, you start displacing your old mindset.

Spiritual Detox

A lot of people struggle in life because they are so obsess about figuring out what to do, when to do it and who to do it with. They obsess about these questions so much and for so long that they've lost sight of the most important question.

Believe it or not, there is a question that transcends all of these. The most important question is, was and always will be "Why?"

Think about it. If you don't know why you're here, then all the technical knowledge in the world won't do you any good. You'll still feel empty, directionless and purposeless. It will all seem, at a certain stand point, empty, shallow and pointless.

It often takes just one bad day for all of this to come crashing down around you. It is no surprise that a lot of people feel lonely in a crowd. It is not all that shocking to discover that a lot of people feel depressed.

They deal with these issues in varying shades of socially acceptable ways. In our society, it's socially acceptable to cheat on your partner when you feel a deep and profound personal existential loneliness. You fill this hole in your soul with sex and you confuse physical intimacy with spiritual intimacy and fulfillment.

The same goes with drinking and, to a certain degree, drugs. But let's get real here: they're all coping mechanisms. Few and far between are the people who see this issue for what it is. All these are a reflection of a spiritual lack. Due to spiritual pollution, we have lost our sense of purpose.

Spiritual detox: Identify your purpose

I know this sounds shocking. But everybody's got purpose. That's right. You've been put on this planet for a reason. You're not just a random collection of cells. You're not just a cluster of tissue. There is something to you that is intrinsically important.

I know you feel small. I know you feel voiceless, powerless, inconsequential. But the truth is you have a purpose. The problem is most people refuse to own up to this. The truth is we all have a sense of purpose.

Maybe sex is your sense of purpose. Maybe drugs gives you purpose. Maybe making more money is your purpose. But the fact that you are acting and setting goals and planning based on something you can not see right now means that you are capable of living in a purposeful way. It may not be the right one. It may not even be optimal. It may even lead to dead ends and further frustration and depression.

Still, there is that power to operate from a sense of purpose. Ask yourself this question. "What is my purpose right here, right now?" Is it sex? Money? Drugs? People's validation? Living up to your parent's expectations? Trying to impress other people? What is it?

Now for the key question

Ask yourself this key question, "Now that I have a clear idea of the laundry list of purposes that I've given myself, does it make sense to me?"

I want you to wrap your mind around this question and think about this deeply. You know what's operating. You know what's animating it. You have to be completely honest about it. But now you have to ask yourself, "Does it serve my purpose?"

How do you know this? What kind of map or compass do you need? Well, it's very simple. You just have to ask a follow up question, "Do these purposes lead to the life that I want for myself and my family?"

If your purpose is drugs, does it lead to the life that you want for you and the ones you love? If your purpose is sex, does it lead to those things? Be completely honest with yourself. Let me cut straight to the chase. If you're reading this book with any kind of honesty, the obvious answer is no!

You're not happy. You're feeling stuck at some level or other. You feel like a liar, a hypocrite. You feel defective, flawed. Now we're making progress. Now you realize that something is missing.

Identifying spiritual pollutants

What are the spiritual toxins weighing you down? Do you constantly compare yourself to other people? Do you open Facebook and look at the timelines of your friends and compare your life to theirs? Do you feed your mind with all sorts of junk like celebrity gossip and political drama?

Do you check out your Twitter feed with a sense of envy or dread in mind? Do you feel left behind when you look at other people's lives in social media? Do they seem so much richer, prettier and more alive than you?

Does it seem like everybody else has a tremendous amount of freedom while you are feeling stuck, frustrated and desperate? Do you constantly compare what's missing in your life with other people's brightest and happiest moments?

Do you find it hard to listen to people sharing pain in their lives without constantly butting in and sharing how you have suffered too?

If any of these questions resonate with you, please understand that they are symptoms of spiritual pollution. You are suffering from them precisely because you feed yourself spiritual poison.

Identify your personal list of spiritual toxins

Any kind of detoxification must begin with the toxins you're trying to get out of your system. The same applies to spiritual detox. Here's the problem. I can't help you all that much in this area. Why? Everybody's list of spiritual toxins is different.

Some people are driven by sex, power and prestige. Others are driven by social approval and living up to certain standards set by others around them. Others are driven by fear, pride, stubbornness. There's really no one size fits all solution here. So I'm not even going to try.

We're all different people from all different backgrounds with all sorts of different experiences. I can go on and on about the things that separate us. Unfortunately, these areas of separation and distinction play a big role in how out spiritual toxins are shaked and positioned in our lives.

What I can suggest to you

I can, however, suggest to you that you reach deep down inside and ask yourself what your spiritual toxins are. Sometimes, you have to ask a question in many different ways to get to the truth. If you've ever gone to a police interrogation or you watched detective movies, you would notice that they would ask basically the same question intended to get the same answer in many different ways.

They do that for 2 reasons. First, they know that people are often confused. They mean to say something, but they really can't quite say it in the right way. So they have to chip away at the different ways of phrasing something until they're clear that you actually mean certain things.

The other reason is more obvious. They're looking for inconsistencies. In other words, they're looking for lies and deception. You should do the same with yourself. Ask yourself the same essential question but in many different ways. Here are some suggested questions.

Ultimately, they're all about identifying your spiritual toxins. Ask the following, "What makes me stubborn? What makes me cling to an idea because of personal pride? What makes me afraid? What makes me feel small and limited? What makes me feel unloved? What do I have a tough time forgiving?"

Believe it or not, we hang on to a lot of these things. I know it sounds counter-intuitive. I mean, after all, who wants to hang on to a brutal memory of a father that used to beat you all the time? Who wants to hang on to that image of your father slapping your mother around? Who wants that?

But the problem is it's like a train wreck. You know you shouldn't look at it. But you can't turn away. You can't look away even if you tried. It doesn't take a rocket scientist or a brain surgeon to figure out that none of this is doing us any favors.

They suck our spiritual life and instead of living life with a tremendous amount of adventure, possibility, purpose and curiosity, we retreat to the tried and proven. We shrink back to the familiar.

It's very lonely in the shadows. So come up with your list. Deep down inside, you already know the answer.

Step #3: Let go of your spiritual pollutants

If your Facebook feed is causing you to continue thinking in a certain way that makes you feel small, spiteful or vindictive, you might want to sit up and pay attention. Please understand that what you're feeling has nothing to do with your friend in New Zealand, Great Britain or in the tropics.

Instead, it has everything to do with you. Whatever negativity you are feeling comes from you. You are just reading into that stimuli. It could be somebody else. It could be somebody living in Iceland or Green Land and you will find something to be envious about because it reflects what you feel is missing in your life.

Similarly, if the people you hang out with tend to bring out the gossip in you or tend to bring out the critique or hater, you might want to open your eyes to this reality. If the kind of books and music you consume always makes you wish that you were somebody else, living a better life, doing better things with your time, you might want to think twice.

I want you to come up with a long laundry list of the things that you normally do that trigger negative mindsets or things that don't spiritually sit well with you.

Step #4: Turn your back on spiritual junk food

I've got some great news, spiritual detox does not involve cold turkey. If you've ever struggled with trying to quit smoking, you know exactly what I'm talking about. Let's get real here. It would be impossible for most people to quit the first time they tried.

I'm not saying that cold turkey doesn't work. It does. It worked for me. But you have to try again and again. When it comes to spiritual junk food or toxins, the better approach is to incrementally, or in a step by step way, pull back from the things that normally trigger you and make you feel small, petty and resentful.

Do you spend a lot of time checking other people's photos on Instagram and imagining yourself living their lives? You might want to cut back on that. Do you spend a lot of time comparing yourself to your friend's travel photos on Facebook or Flickr, you might want to give that a break.

Please understand that you shouldn't go through a complete break where you let go of these immediately. I'm telling you, if you try to do that, it's just not going to happen. Instead, gradually realize that you're doing these things.

Be aware of what you're doing. You're not making the envy, resentment and frustration go away. Instead, you're feeding it. And the more you realize that and the clearer everything becomes, you will find the strength to do what you need to do. This is how you feel empowered.

The bottom line is you have to realize and say to yourself, "When I do these things, it brings out the worst in me."

Get your moment of truth

Everybody who's ever gone through a life changing episode goes through a moment of truth. It is that time when the alcoholic wakes up in a pile of vomit at the bottom of a public toilet. It is that time when a drug addict wakes up in an ambulance on the way to the emergency room. It is that time when an unfaithful girlfriend has a gun drawn to her face by the partner of the guy she's messing with.

Everybody's got a moment of truth. Imagine what your moment of truth would be like if you continue to suck up all that spiritual pollution. The good news it shouldn't take much imagination.

After all, you're reading this book because you're unhappy. You're reading this book because at some point in your life, you're feeling stuck.

Get your sense of urgency

Now that you have blown up the emotional pain, fear, that sense of loss and regret of what you're doing in your life, use these to push you to make the necessary changes. Use them to push you to look at your life differently and the things that you choose to entertain yourself with, the people who you hang out with, the beliefs that you keep playing in the back of your head, get that push because nobody's going to push you.

Everybody will always try to kiss your ass. In this context, friends are the worst. Why? They try to comfort you. That's their instinct. That's what friends are for, right? But the problem is you don't need a friend right now. Instead, you need somebody to tell you the truth and nothing but the truth.

You need somebody who would light the fire underneath your feet so you can get moving. Otherwise, it's too easy to just fall for reassurance because, after all, there will be another day, right? The problem with tomorrow and getting things done tomorrow is that tomorrow never comes. You have to do it now.

Chapter 9

Holistic Detox

I've focused on the most important stuff

Have you noticed that up to this point I haven't talked about physical detox? It's because physical detox is the least of your worries. The physical issues that you may have, the financial problems that you are struggling with, the sexual issues that you may be grappling with, all of these are just icing on the cake. This is the tip of the iceberg. I'm focused on what really matters, which is your mental, emotional, and spiritual state. Fix those and the tip of the iceberg changes dramatically. Fix what's inside and the outside will take care of itself. Whatever it is you're struggling and whatever bad habits you may have are just all emanations and manifestations of things going on deep down inside and this is why this detox system works from the inside out. I'm not saying that I will completely disregard the need for physical detox but it's just one part of the equation.

Start with a mental detox

Adopt meditation and mindfulness practices. Try these three. You can easily find guides on these meditation/mindfulness techniques online. I've listed these three since they are the most effective for me.

1: Count your breath
2. Present object observation or single object observation
3. Transcendental meditation

Use your increased mental focus to separate your feelings from your external stimuli. You don't have to get upset when your girlfriend says you're a loser. You don't have to immediately feel sad when you remember your mother abandoning your family for another man. You don't have to go off the deep end when that mental image of your boss verbally humiliating you in front of three hundred people flashes into your mind. Learn how to separate stimuli from habitual mental interpretation through mindfulness and meditation.

Emotional detox

Actively let go or neutralize negative emotions. When you see, hear, or detect something that the emotionally triggers you, consciously come up with an opposite reaction. For example, you're scrolling through your Facebook feed and you noticed that your ex-boyfriend now has a new girlfriend and she is a thousand times prettier than you. When you detect that spark of anger, resentment, and hate or envy because he's moved on, quickly counteract it with feeling happy for him, feeling happy for her. Share their joy. In Buddhism, depression is almost impossible because one of the skills you learn as a Buddhist is to share other people's joy. Be grateful for them.

Practice gratitude

Be grateful for what you have. You may be on your deathbed in a hospital room with stage 4 cancer. Be thankful that you still can breathe. Be thankful that you can still have time even though it's very short. Be thankful that you have one final chance to put everything together so you go out with some sense of meaning and purpose. Whatever it is, be thankful. It's hard to find unhappy person who is also ungrateful. It's almost impossible.

Mentally detox by being in the moment

Mentally and spiritually detox by being in the moment. Transcendental meditation is good for this because TM melts your thoughts. You're not agonizing about things that happened in the past. All that is pointless because you can't change the facts of the past. The past is the past. It already happened. By the same token, you're not beating yourself up unnecessarily about things that have yet to happen. Why worry? It hasn't happened yet. Instead, you've trained yourself to focus on the moment. There's nobody to become. There's nothing to apologize for. There's nothing to be. There are no people to please. There's no need to be validated. You just are. Let that sink in. Tap the power of just being. There's nothing to compare yourself to. There's nothing to live up to. There's just the present moment. Let go of everything else.

Unleash the Power of Fasting

When it comes to physical detox, nothing beats fasting. Seriously. That's the bottom line.

Fasting Explained

Fasting is essentially letting go of solid food. Whether you stop eating for one day or forty days, it's all about letting go of solid food. That's the classic definition of fasting. I suggest that you adopt a fast. There are many different variations of this.

Different variations of physical fasting

You can do the classical fast, which is water only. You can do the juice fast. You can do the Daniel fast of the Hebrew Bible.

Classic fast

Classic fasting simply means you drink only water. However, don't think that you're not eating when you are fasting. You may not be eating physical food but you must eat spiritual food. This is why I suggest that you adopt a meditation practice, that you keep a journal, and that you watch what you feed your head while you're going through a fast.

Feed your head inspirational things that push you to become a bigger and better person than who you think you are. Feed on things that break down your ego and crush your pride. Feed on things that destroy your ears and fill you with a tremendous sense of possibility. These are all mental and spiritual food. The great thing about fasting is that it enables you to hunger for this type of food so the sustenance that you get becomes more important than physical sustenance that preserves your bones, tissues and blood.

- The juice fast
There are many different variations of juice fasts. I suggest that you drink juice that is not all that sugary and satisfying. It should have some taste but that's all. The whole point here is not to get distracted by the syrupy goodness of your juice. Instead, it should have a little bit of flavor and a little bit of calories but not really all that different from water.

Remember: when you're fasting, you are aligning your physical detoxification and letting go of physical toxins in your fat cells and blood with the detoxification happening in your mind and spirit. They have to line up and this is how you regain your sense of integrity and wholeness.

The Daniel fast

The Daniel fast is simply letting go of the most common foods that you eat and just eating only a specific type of food. The classic Daniel fast from the Hebrew Bible is eating only vegetables but you can use the keto version of the Daniel fast meaning you eat only eggs are high-fat foods and zero carbs. If you're looking to lose weight and also turbocharge detoxification, the keto modifications of the Daniel fast can do wonders.

Time your fast right

If you are doing any kind of fast that involves ingesting calories, I am, of course, talking about the juice fast or the Daniel fast, time your ingestion properly. One way to boost the effects that you get from holistic detoxification is to ingest calories only once a day. It's going to be very hard at first but when it kicks, it's a beautiful thing because the discipline that you pick you up while you are fasting and going through detox will help you for the rest of your life. You become a more disciplined and focused person.

Keep repeating your detox schedule. If you're able to pull off a one-day or two-day detox, keep repeating it. Practiced makes perfect. Repetition ensures that whatever insights and whatever freedom you have achieved will eventually start to kick in. Eventually, it will become permanent. The key is to keep going through this fasting and detox process.

Scale up when it becomes comfortable

Once you think that things have gotten easy regarding the type of fasting you're doing, scale it up in terms of intensity or kind. For example, you started out with the Daniel fast for three days, try to get to ten days then twenty-one days. Once you've mastered the Daniel fast, then move on to juice fast. Scale that up and then go to a classic fast. There's always room for improvement.

Conclusion

If you are weighed down, frustrated, or feeling stuck, please understand that it's all an illusion. You're feeling stuck because you think you're stuck. You're feeling powerless because you imagine yourself to be lacking power.

Do yourself a big favor and start making new choices, and the best choice that you can make is to detoxify your mind, spirit, and body. Follow the tips outlined in this book and scale up conscientiously and you'd be surprised as to how far you can go. You'd be surprised as to how capable you truly are as a human being.

Author kol tov

www.ingramcontent.com/pod-product-compliance
Lightning Source LLC
Chambersburg PA
CBHW050907290526
45792CB00002B/723